Growing Readers

Purchased with Smart Start Funds

Thoughts and Feelings

Thoughts and Feelings

Afraid

Written by Susan Riley
Photos by David M. Budd

The Child's World®, Inc.

Published by The Child's World®, Inc.

Copyright © 2000 by The Child's World®, Inc.
All rights reserved. No part of this book may be
reproduced or utilized in any form or by any means
without written permission from the publisher.
Printed in the United States of America.

Design and Production:
The Creative Spark, San Juan Capistrano, CA

Photos: © 1998 David M. Budd Photography
        Corbis/George Lepp, page 17

Library of Congress Cataloging-in-Publication Data

Riley, Susan, 1946–
      Afraid / by Susan Riley.
          p. cm. — (Thoughts and feelings)
      Summary: Simple rhyming text describes fear, how it feels, and what
can cause it.
      ISBN 1-56766-666-3 (lib. bdg. : alk. paper)
      1. Fear in children Juvenile literature. [1. Fear.] I. Title. II. Series.
BF723.F4R55   1999
152.4'6—dc21   99-25376
                                                                                CIP

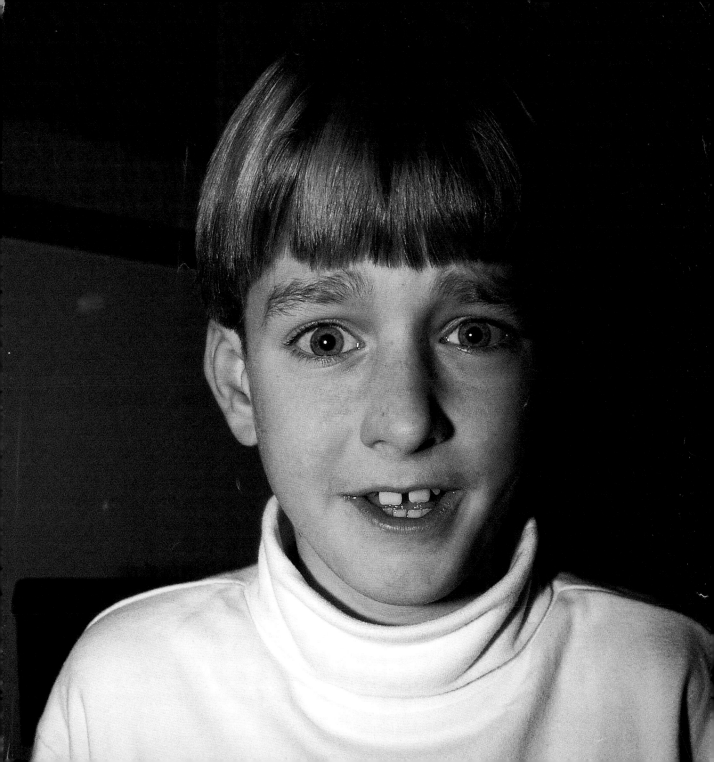

Here, behind the door,
it's me.
I don't want to come out.
I'm afraid, you see.

Have you been afraid?
Everyone has, they say.

Let me tell you some things
that make me that way.

Sometimes alone
in my bed late at night,
I'm afraid of the dark,
so I turn on the light.

And once when I climbed up
a tree that was tall,
I was afraid to come down,
afraid I would fall.

I'm afraid
when I have
to go get a
shot, I'm
afraid it
will hurt—

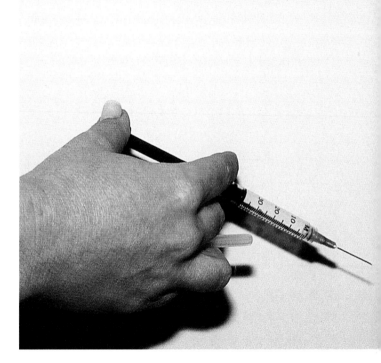

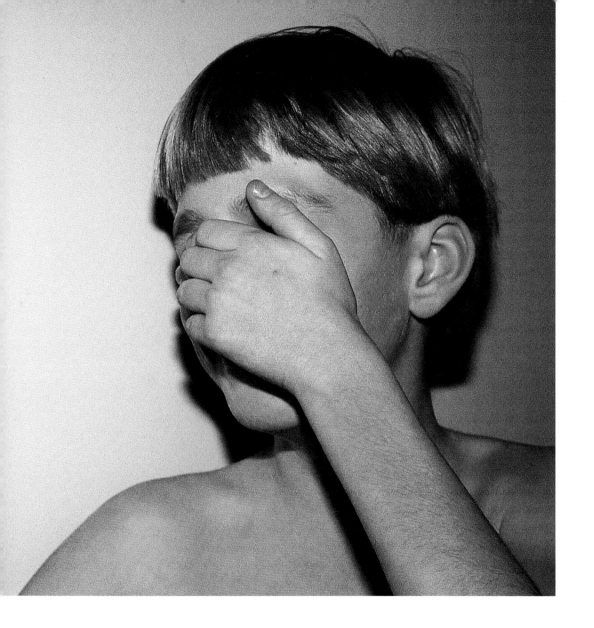

hurt a whole lot.

15

And I'm afraid of storms,

of thunder and lightning.

Yes, storms can be very, very frightening.

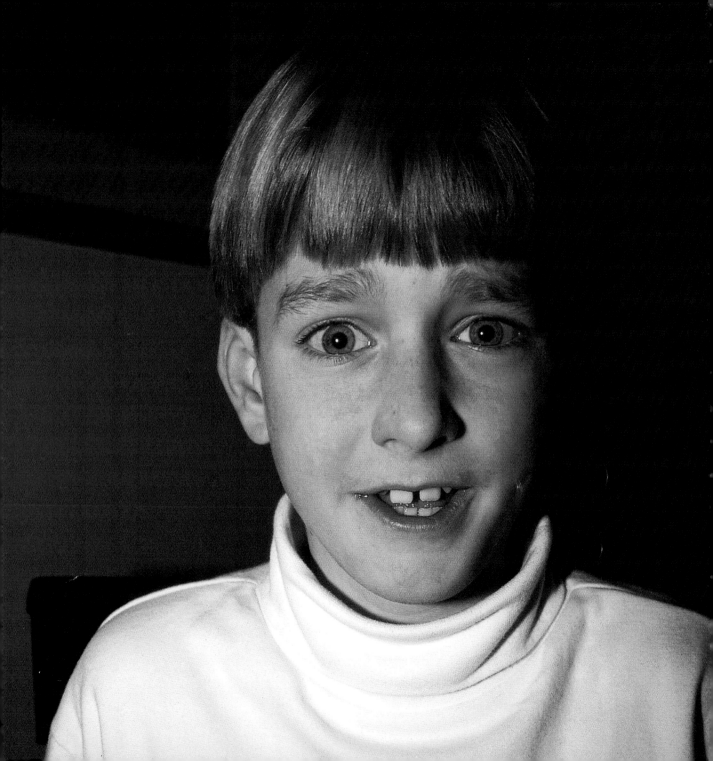

Doing things for the first time
makes me

AFRAID...

like my first day of school,

my first scary book,
and my first parade.

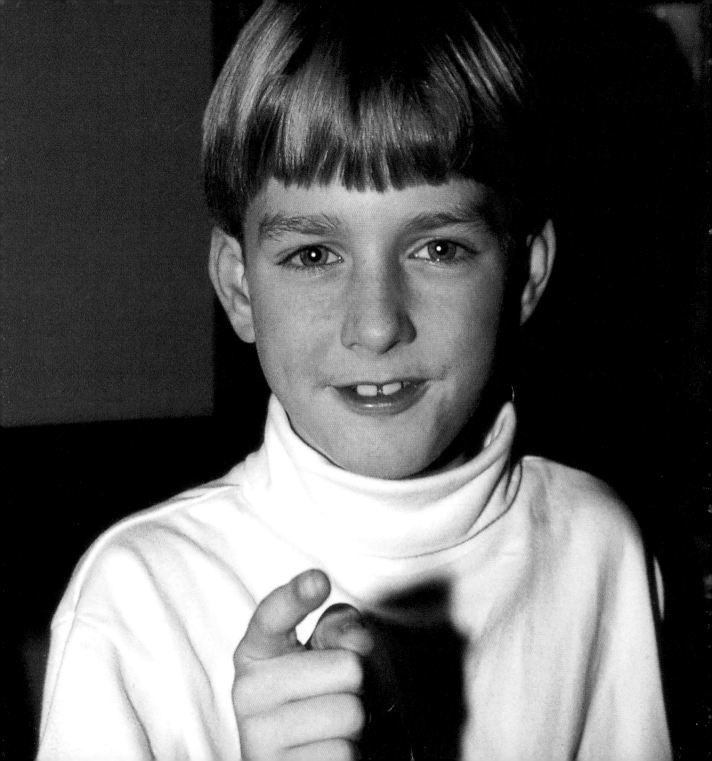

What makes you afraid,
or scares you the most?

Being lost? Big dogs?
Or monsters and ghosts?

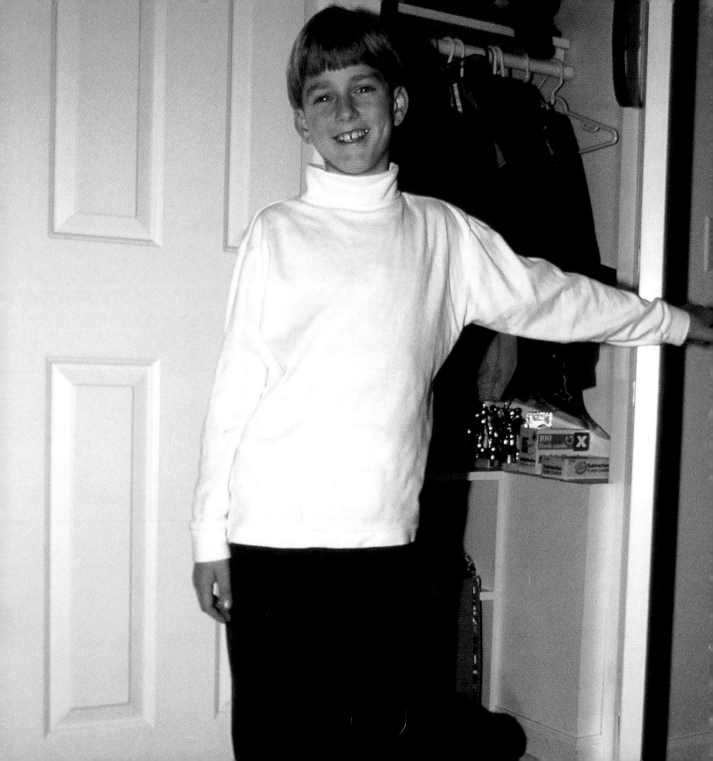

Now that I've talked about it,
I'm not afraid anymore.
So I'll come out from hiding
behind the big door.
And if you talk about
things you're afraid to do,
you will feel much better, too.

For Further Information and Reading

Books

Senter, Ruth Hollinger. *Annie Ashcroft Looks into the Dark.* Minneapolis, MN: Bethany House, 1998.

Stanek, Muriel. *All Alone After School.* Morton Grove, IL: Albert Whitman & Co., 1998.

Carlson, Nancy. *Harriet's Recital.* Minneapolis, MN: First Avenue Editions, 1997.

Web Sites

For information about thoughts and feelings:
http://www.kidshealth.org/kid/feeling/

Tips on what to do when you're all alone:
http://www.cfc-efc.ca/docs/00000724.htm

Fairy tales and stories about thoughts and feelings from all over the world: http://www.familyinternet.com/StoryGrowby/